The
Hidden Rainbow

The
Hidden
Rainbow

COLOUR TO HEAL

KELLY DORJI

Illustrations by the author

PENGUIN BOOKS

An imprint of Penguin Random House

PENGUIN BOOKS

USA | Canada | UK | Ireland | Australia
New Zealand | India | South Africa | China

Penguin Books is part of the Penguin Random House group of companies
whose addresses can be found at global.penguinrandomhouse.com

Published by Penguin Random House India Pvt. Ltd.
4th Floor, Capital Tower 1, MG Road,
Gurugram 122 002, Haryana, India

First published in Penguin Books by Penguin Random House India 2019

Text and illustrations copyright © Kelly Dorji 2019

10 9 8 7 6 5 4 3

ISBN 9780143446569

For sale in the Indian Subcontinent only

Book design and layout by Akangksha Sarmah
Typeset in Didot eText Std, Nuptial Script Lt Pro,
Printed at Replika Press Pvt. Ltd, India

www.penguin.co.in

f o r

Her Majesty Gyalyum
Dorji Wangmo Wangchuck
Queen Mother of Bhutan

*There cannot be enduring peace, prosperity, equality
and brotherhood in this world if our aims are so separate
and divergent, if we do not accept that in the end we are people,
all alike, sharing the earth among ourselves and also with
other sentient beings, all of whom have an equal role and
stake in the state of this planet and its players.*

*——His Majesty Jigme Khesar Namgyel Wangchuck
King of Bhutan*

Thimphu, Bhutan, 20 February 2004

From the Author

In this age of individualism and increased stress, many of us are turning inwards. This return to spirituality is, perhaps, hope for a better future for us all. Colouring and the use of colours have, for a while now, been an effective form of therapy. My journey of two and a half years in creating this design work of spiritual fiction was inspired by Buddhist iconography and my love for Guru Padmasambhava.

It is not my intention to teach Buddhism or spirituality to anyone. In fact, I am merely transmitting my understanding of the roots of the Dharma and my own spiritual journey through visual representations of Buddhist iconography in Bhutan.

It is my wish that you enjoy this book as a source of comfort by simply adding colour to it, or you could perhaps go deeper and research the origins of my inspiration. I come from a land of rainbows, a land that is sacred with its hues of mysticism, legends and kings.

I pray that you too may experience this and find your inner rainbow as you find deeper meaning in my work for yourself.

Tashi Delek!

Kelly Dorji,
Thimphu, Bhutan

This book was completed with a great sense of joy and gratitude for the blessings I have enjoyed as a Bhutanese, and in my limited knowledge and service of the Dharma. I offer prayers for the long lives of Their Majesties the King and Queen of Bhutan and His Royal Highness the Gyalsey, and I offer endless prayers and gratitude for the long life of His Majesty the Great Fourth King of Bhutan. My prayers of gratitude for the affection and kindness of Her Majesty the Dharma Queen, Ashi Kesang Choden Wangchuck, The Royal Grand Mother of Bhutan. My prayers and gratitude for Her Majesty the Gyalyum Queen Mother Ashi Dorji Wangmo Wangchuck, to whom I dedicate this book, for graciously keeping an eye on my upbringing. My prayers for Her Royal Highness Ashi Kesang Wangmo Wangchuck, who illuminates the path of compassion wherever she goes.

I thank my father, brothers and sisters for their love and support. My late brother Tashi Namgay is an important part of this book, though he is no longer with us.

I thank Kama Wangdi for his patience in helping me rekindle my love for art. I thank Lam Choeten for his kind guidance and friendship over the years. Thanks to Chhimi Yangdon for encouraging me since the very conception of this book. To Tshering Tashi for all his valuable advice. To Maharani Priyadarshini Raje Scindia for her love and friendship. Thanks to Zuki and Choney for their good work in transforming my unsteady hand into clean images. Thanks to Chand Bhattarai for his support. For their loyalty and love, and the many colouring competitions at the office, I thank Reeta and Swara.

A special thank you to, Mita Kapur, for always being so wonderful. I thank all my friends for putting up with my erratic behaviour for the past two and a half years while I worked two jobs and many a late night to produce this book.

My eternal gratitude goes to Ashi Kesang Choden Tashi (Baby Kesang) for her encouragement, support and positivity in pushing me to give my best and for guiding me with her immense knowledge of the Dharma.

This book would not have been possible without the unconditional love of my mother, Louise Dorji.

Foreword

Kelly Dorji is not only an artist but also a versatile individual who understands the multifaceted aspects of art that manifest as hope and beauty in one's life.

The Hidden Rainbow took many months of gruelling research and revisions.

I have been fortunate enough to get a glimpse of both Kelly's artistic journey and his personal spiritual journey that has led to this wonderful work of love and sincere determination. Kelly's discovering and developing his artwork, as well as uncovering his connection with the divine, was an inspiring and touching process to bear witness to.

Art is timeless and eternal, in that it is an expression of the self through symbolism. Though these symbols used in *The Hidden Rainbow* may be Buddhist in their origins, it is truly for all those who believe in the divine, the humanity and the innate goodness that is inherent in every single being.

I am grateful to Kelly Dorji for allowing me to accompany him on this wonderful journey. And it is my sincere hope and aspiration that anyone that connects with the book and its meaning will be able to find inspiration, hope, compassion and universal love in their lives.

Tashi Delek!

May All Auspicious Signs Manifest!

Kesang Choden Tashi
Thimphu, Bhutan

A GUIDE TO THE USE OF COLOURS AND THEIR SYMBOLISM IN BUDDHISM:

The main colours used in Buddhist art are blue, black, white, red, green and yellow. With black as the exception, the other five colours are representative of a specific Buddha in the depiction of the five Wisdom Buddhas of the Vajrayana or Tantric Tradition of Buddhism.

The colour **B L U E** is used to represent the Healing Buddha, signifying calm, purity and healing.

W H I T E signifies purity and is the colour of knowledge and longevity. The primordial Buddha 'Vairocana' is depicted in white.

The Buddha Amitabha is shown in **R E D**, which symbolizes life and holiness.

The Amoghasiddhi Buddha in **G R E E N** signifies accomplishment and the elimination of envy.

Y E L L O W is the colour chosen to depict Ratnasambhava, who is a symbol of balance and humility.

Through meditation, these colours may contribute to the restorative process of the human condition by transforming human delusions to original qualities as follows:

- Meditating on the colour blue can pacify aggression.

- White can transform ignorance into wisdom.

- Red turns attachment into selflessness and realization.

- Concentrating on green can eliminate jealousy.

- Meditation on the colour yellow can enrich the sense of self and eliminate pride.

*om
is the
centre*

*S*piritually, the concept of 'Om' represents everything. The sound represents three different tones. The chant is an effective tool to bring awareness and heighten energy levels in the body. The 'ah' sound represents creation and is the beginning of all sounds. This sound is produced in the throat and the back of the mouth where the tongue is rooted and reverberates in the lower abdomen.

The 'oo' sound is significant of universal energy and comes from between the tongue and the palate up to the lips and reverberates in the solar plexus.

The 'mm' sound signifies changing energies. This sound reverberates in the crown of the head.

Chanting 'Om' gives a sense of continuity and these three distinct sounds combine to drive the awareness of breath in the body.

You will find that I have depicted beauty all over this illustration because it is always a wonderful experience to chant 'Om' before meditating. It has taught me that 'Ommani Péhmeh Hoong', ultimately, is the duality of method and wisdom. It may be understood as the seizing of wisdom by method and the seizing of method by wisdom.

I wish for you to be able to nourish the 'Om' in your centre as well!

'Now this, monks, is the noble truth of stress: Birth is stressful, ageing is stressful, death is stressful; sorrow, lamentation, pain, distress and despair are stressful; association with the unloved is stressful, separation from the loved is stressful, not getting what is wanted is stressful. In short, the five clinging-aggregates are stressful.'

~ The Buddha

dukkha

An important Buddhist concept is the truth of suffering or 'Dukkha'. Known as the First Noble Truth, suffering afflicts us in many ways, according to the first three sights the Buddha saw on his maiden journey outside his palace. These sights were that of old age, sickness and death. The root of suffering goes much deeper, says the Buddha. Many happenings in our lives often fail to live up to our expectations. And even when we are able to satisfy our desires, we only feel temporary relief, as cravings are an unending cycle. For many, this truth is a realism that is neither optimistic nor pessimistic. The Buddha's teachings guide us towards ending all suffering.

The footprint, as depicted alongside, represents my experience and the act of travelling through life in the human form. We must experience all the elements and create memory and attachment as depicted in the cloud throne. Our lives are adorned with material comforts as well as nourished with love and beauty.

Never a man did destiny book,
That never did he to destiny look.

phurba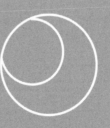

The Second Noble Truth is known as Samudāya, which means 'the cause of suffering' arising from clinging to desires. The Buddha taught that the cause of all suffering is 'tanhā' or desire. These are defined as greed, ignorance or hatred, also referred to as the 'three poisons'.

The 'Phurba' is the three-sided dagger widely believed to have been invented by Guru Padmasambhava. It is attributed to an ancient Vedic tool used to pin down sacrifices. The three segments represent the power of the phurba to transform negative energies.

Subdue the three poisons of greed, ignorance and hatred with the 'Phurba' at your side and transcend chakras to attain inner peace. This is signifies of your inner strength to overcome adverse situations or conditions in your lives. I used my inner 'Phurba' as a teenager in my tryst with drugs, and I have since privately used this victory to encourage addicts and alcoholics to search for the inner strength to overcome their afflictions.

nirhodha

*T*o end his suffering, the Buddha spent six years in discovery and meditation. In his realization, the Buddha became aware of an end to suffering, and that it was limitless. This was known as the Third Noble Truth or 'Nirhodha'.

The Buddha taught that humans who are less dependent on desire, ill will and ignorance are more likely to end suffering.

The fruits of the Third Noble Truth are said to be perfect wisdom and great compassion.

In the illustration alongside, I have designed the background to compliment the bhumisparsa mudra hand position that the Buddha is using. Lord Buddha is said to have used this gesture when he attained enlightenment and it invokes the earth to bear witness.

*The clarity we seek is only
blurred by the screen of expectation.
Drop it and deal with the anchor of regret.
Drop it and sail in the moment.*

epiphany

*T*he path that leads to the cessation of suffering is the Fourth Noble Truth. When the Buddha attained enlightenment through meditation, he realized that an extreme way of life was fruitless. The Buddha taught that the way to happiness was to avoid extremes and, instead, follow a moderate way of life. This he referred to as the 'Middle Path'.

In learning about the causes and nature of suffering, the Buddha prescribed its cure, known to us as the Noble Eightfold Path.

Good conduct, mental development and wisdom envelop these eight steps to end all suffering, and we will revisit them later, when we journey to discover our hidden rainbows!

'Ka' invokes Kamadeva.
'La' invokes Indra, the ruler of Heaven.
'Ee' signifies satisfaction.
'Mm' invokes all that bring happiness and love.

love

What Eros is to Greeks and Cupid was to Romans, Kamadeva is to Hindus. Lord Shiva had decided to become an ascetic after the tragic demise of his first wife, Sati. A demon called Tarakasura took advantage of this upon earning two boons from Lord Brahma. His first wish was that no one could destroy him and his second wish was that only the son of Lord Shiva would be able to kill him. This made him very powerful as Shiva had decided to never remarry or have children. Tarakasura unleashed terror in heaven, hell and on earth. The only solution was to get Lord Shiva to break his vow of celibacy and have a child. So they appealed to Kamadeva. He accompanied Goddess Parvati to Mount Kailash, where Lord Shiva was deep in meditation and shot his arrow of desire at Lord Shiva's heart. Lord Shiva awoke from his meditation and was mesmerized by Parvati's beauty, until he realized that he had been tricked. Angered at being deceived, Lord Shiva destroyed Kamadeva. Parvati begged Shiva to spare Kamadeva, so he was revived but without form. Lord Shiva and Goddess Parvati had a son, Kartikeya, who went on to destroy Tarakasura. In the illustration alongside, subdued by Shiva, Kamadeva remains eternally present behind the face of death.

It is said that the chanting of the Kleem Mantra can invoke love, material satisfaction and worldly comforts.

free

your

mind

Chidākāsha or space of consciousness is the key to visualization, which binds us with the conscious, subconscious and super-conscious.

Meditation is the art of being able to free your mind in order to gain control of it. Meditation is believed to give us more rest than the deepest sleep that you can ever have. When the mind is free from distraction and becomes calm, it is meditating.

Our own minds are our greatest assets or our worst enemies. A key to meditation is to recognize that you are only a witness. Without training our minds to let thoughts come and go, we are at the mercy of our instincts.

As sentient beings practise meditation to attain Buddhahood and shine from within among cloud thrones, it is the resolve of the Dorji (Thunderbolt) that binds the past with the future.

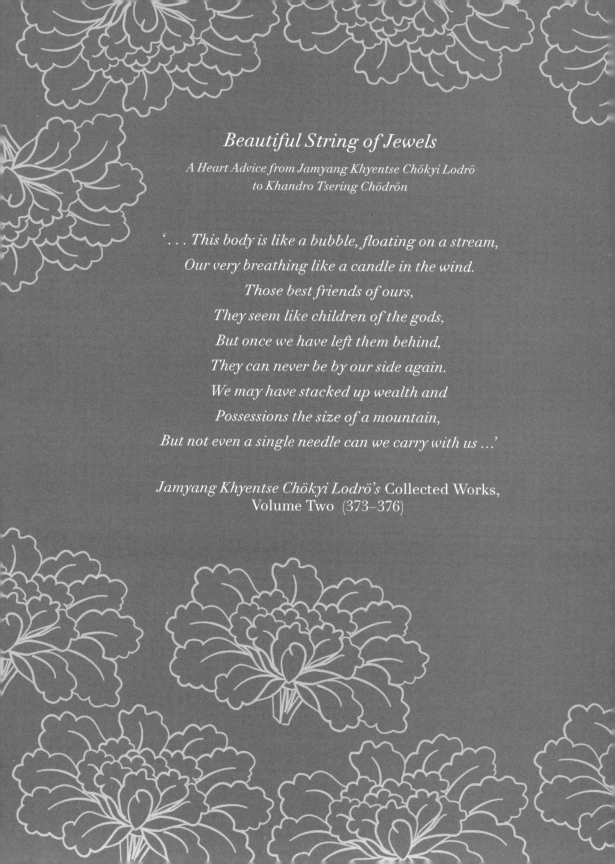

Beautiful String of Jewels

*A Heart Advice from Jamyang Khyentse Chökyi Lodrö
to Khandro Tsering Chödrön*

'... *This body is like a bubble, floating on a stream,
Our very breathing like a candle in the wind.
Those best friends of ours,
They seem like children of the gods,
But once we have left them behind,
They can never be by our side again.
We may have stacked up wealth and
Possessions the size of a mountain,
But not even a single needle can we carry with us ...*'

Jamyang Khyentse Chökyi Lodrö's Collected Works,
Volume Two (373–376)

cloud
thrones

*I*n Buddhist art, cloud thrones are depicted to seat deities, lamas and gurus. Afloat on billowing clouds, these cloud thrones illustrated alongside are also inspired by the Greek Etimasia or the empty throne. In Ancient Greek representation, it signified Zeus, head of the gods, and in early Buddhist art, it stood for the Buddha.

Memory and tribute flow through the summing up of the elements and knowledge to rest in time upon cloud thrones.

the
rainbow
body of
light

I read that when His Eminence Dzogchen Khenpo Choga Rinpoche's teacher, Dzogchen Lama Karma Rinpoche, passed away in 2013, his human frame of five feet nine inches shrank to about twenty inches in the following ten days.

A fully enlightened soul can liberate the body into three levels. The Rainbow Body that occurs after death is the first level of this phenomenon. The next step is referred to as the Rainbow Body of Light. Signs begin to appear of this while one is still alive. Eventually, the body will shrink over time and disappear in a flash of light.

The highest and most rare form of this enlightenment is the Rainbow Body of Great Transference. Here, the yogi's body not only dissolves completely into light but also remains visible.

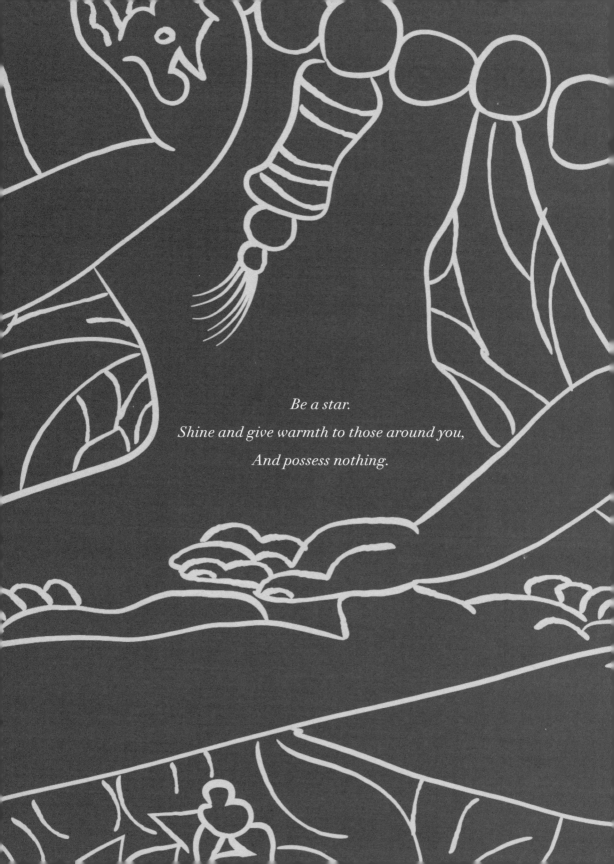

Be a star.
Shine and give warmth to those around you,
And possess nothing.

108

*T*he earliest records on the use of prayer beads are from around 3000 BC. by the ancient Egyptians. 'Bead' is derived from the Anglo-Saxon 'bede', meaning 'prayer'.

In Buddhism, prayer beads are used to count the number of times a mantra is recited. Traditionally, these 'malas' number 108, signifying a spiritual connection with the universe. A full-length prayer bead has counter beads which divide the mala into four sections of twenty-seven beads each.

the eight-fold path and the eight lucky signs

orrect understanding or Right View is important as it is related to seeing everything in the world as it is, not as we believe it to be. In the book *Old Path White Clouds: Walking in the Footsteps of the Buddha*, Thich Nhat Hanh quotes Lord Buddha as saying, 'I must state clearly that my teaching is a method to experience reality and not reality itself, just as a finger pointing at the moon is not the moon itself.' By this, the Buddha seems to have never intended his followers to blindly follow his teachings but, instead, practise them and then judge for themselves.

Like the eternal knot alongside, the recurring theme of using double images in some of the lucky signs depicted in this book symbolizes the duality of life.

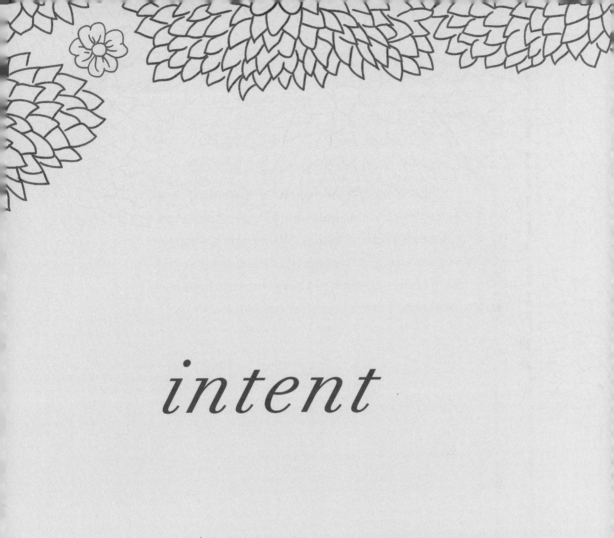

intent

*I*t is important for humans to conduct themselves with right intentions and compassion towards other living beings.

The Dungkar or conch is associated with heralding the Dharma and awakening followers to work for the welfare of all sentient beings. The conch is depicted with flower patterns and is wrapped in the flowing energy and goodwill of the silk scarf. I believe that enlightenment can also be attained through perfect compassion alone.

speak
right

*I*n ignorance, very often we do not realize the effect that our words have on others. Sometimes, we utter words and then immediately regret having said them. Words, once uttered, enter the unaccountable permanence of existence. If you were to be conscious of your intent, then you can control your speech and its effect on others. By consciously stopping yourself from speaking in anger, you will build a habit of compassion.

The lucky fish symbolize duality and harmony. These 'Sernya' (a pair of golden fish) cooperate and flourish in freedom and fidelity. Originally, the two fish are said to have symbolized the Ganges and Yamuna rivers in India, but over time, they have come to represent good fortune in Buddhism as well.

act
right

*W*hen you have the right thought and intent, correct actions should follow. Right Action is being ethical and respectful towards everything in life. When we live in consideration of and are compassionate towards the earth and its creatures, we are acting in accordance with co-existence, which benefits all beings. Right Action could also come from putting less strain on resources, stemming from our compassion for the survival of nature.

livelihood

When your actions for livelihood show disregard towards life, your advancement in spirituality is hampered. Buddhism advocates the principle of respect for all life.

The Wheel represents Gautama Buddha and his teachings. The Khorlo will turn continuously in the universe for all beings who are born, die and are reborn under the control of karma and action.

I like the Wheel symbolism because there are endless references to the sun in its depiction in different cultures and histories throughout time. In particular, I love reading about the ancient Egyptian worship of Raa (the Sun God). That is why I have depicted two wheels here, significant of the sun and the earth and their overlapping destinies.

effort

*B*y cultivating enthusiasm through Right Effort, a positive attitude will balance life. Right Effort should be the product of a balanced attitude and positive determination.

The precious parasol or Dhug saves us from all obstacles in this life, such as sickness, contagious diseases, spirit possession, and also from obstacles in the next life. It saves us from being tormented by both temporary and long-term sufferings. It embodies notions of wealth or royalty.

mindfulness

*R*ight Mindfulness makes you a witness to your own thoughts and perceptions by being aware of the present moment, however fleeting it may be. This means being focused in the moment. It is the awareness of the continuous present.

Right Mindfulness is being aware of the journey and to be clear and undistracted at any given moment. It forms the foundations of meditation.

The Gyaltsen or Victory Banner symbolizes the Buddha's teachings. It denotes the Buddha's conquest over the hindrances of pride, desire, disturbing emotions, and the fear of death.

Use your ability to serve,
Your compassion to love,
And use your excess to comfort.

concentration

C oncentration can be described as a single-pointedness of mind. Spiritually speaking, this practice is an ultimate concentration but does not mean we ignore our human instincts or worldly desires. I believe it to indicate that we must balance the focus of consciousness.

The Vase or 'Bumpa' denotes wealth. We have all, at some point, been told that the love of money is the root of all evil. Money and wealth form the roots of our ability, and bad deeds are branches on the tree of our responsibilities.

the hidden
rainbow

*O*ur conscious minds can remain centered, at any given moment, on sight, sound, smell, taste or touch.

The offerings of the five senses alongside are comprised of a mirror (sight), a musical instrument (hearing or sound), incense (smell), fruit (taste) and a silken scarf (touch).

It is through our senses that we experience the world. In spiritual practice, we can mentally or physically enjoy the delights of all our senses with a peaceful mind and thus cause blissful experiences.

Mt Meru, as depicted alongside, is a mythological yet sacred concept said to be the centre of all the physical, metaphysical and spiritual universes. It lies across a cosmic ocean and has always fascinated me, as I particularly enjoy applying this subject to fantasy and science fiction—how I would use it in my stories.

friends

A favourite folktale from Bhutan is about the four harmonious friends. First, a bird plants a seed and a rabbit waters it. A monkey fertilizes it and an elephant protects it. Over time, the seed grows into a tree and bears fruit. The four friends work together to reach and collect the fruit.

I thought it would be fun for you, the colourist, to enjoy some sketching of your own by using the empty prayer flags hanging in the foreground to depict your own wishful seeds and fruits. For instance, I drew a few credit cards in my prayer flags!

the six
symbols of
longevity

*T*he Six Symbols of Longevity appear commonly in Buddhist art. As Buddhism spread to other parts of the world, in China, the image of the old man of long life became a symbol of the deity of longevity. In front of him is a bowl of divine fruit from the eternal peach tree. A conch shell of longevity hangs wrapped in a cloth from his cane. The eternal stream flows in the background as two widely used symbols of longevity, a pair of cranes, bask in the foreground. Another symbol of long life is the deer, said to be the only animal that can locate the plant of immortality. In my design of this classic piece, the raven surveys the scene. The raven is 'Jarog Donchen', an emanation of Mahakala, the principle deity of Bhutan in bird form.

three mythical creatures of harmony

O ften seen on victory banners signifying reconciliation, these six creatures symbolize universal harmony and love, even though they are enemies. The garuda and snowlion are representative of the skies and land, and their union makes up the winged-lion. The otter and fish are traditional enemies but are joined to form the fur-bearing fish. The water-monster or crocodile and the snail make up the makara dragon.

My intention was to design a representation of the reconciliation between the disharmony in the three realms of the skies, surface and underworld.

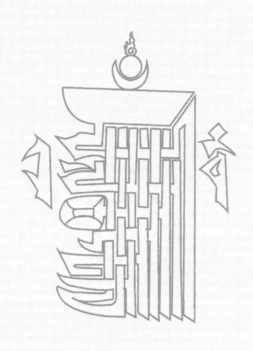

eevam

*T*he most powerful representation of the Tantric Buddhist tradition is the symbol of the Kalachakra. Surrounded by a ring of fire, this combination of seven individual syllables has a crescent, disc and curve on the top. On either side are the characters Ee (emptiness) and Vaam (bliss). Designed in a mirror to reflect the outermost 'circle of wisdom' of the Mandala, my intention is to offer all those who look upon this symbol a sense of empowerment.

A Dharma protector upholds this symbol and the silk scarf at the base stands for peace. The two birds represent the duality of freedom and belonging.

existential

*O*ne's rebirth and existence are determined by deeds or karma. In our cycles of existence, we must pass through all the realms, of which some are more unpleasant than others.

Though some believe that these realms are actual places, many regard them as metaphorical.

My version of the six realms of desire is depicted through six triangles with two more inner triangles depicting karma and passion as an integral part of the entire mandala. This representation is made personal by the central figure of the Dorji (Thunderbolt).

Niraya or Naraka (the Hell Realm) is said to be the most terrible of the six realms. Hell beings are short-tempered. The only way hell beings deal with things that make them angry is through aggression. Does this description remind you of humans of the modern world?

You may like to research the concept of mandala further; it really is a fascinating concept of impermanence.

chakra

I first heard of the secret of the 'wisdom of fire'—Tummo meditation practice—when I was a young boy listening to my grandmother's tales of Lhasa. Passed down in the Vajrayana traditions of Buddhism for the most part of the last nine hundred years, this is an advanced form of meditation whose practitioners are said to be able to spectacularly raise their body temperature and dry wet blankets thrown over their bare bodies.

Our bodies have focal energy points called chakras, and we naturally have this warmth within us in the area below the navel chakra. By visualization, breathing techniques and movement, we can generate our inner heat. On a physical level, this warmth is responsible for the temperature of our body. On an energetic level, the Tummo fire is said to pass through our channels, melting away the subtlest blockages and surging energy throughout the body.

As the flame penetrates each of the main chakras, spreading to all the branches and every pore of our body, the doors to our true nature may be opened.

tranquillity

ollowed by the Buddha himself, this path from calm to insight has become the traditional aim of meditation. It shows us that primary consciousness, though pure, is trapped by habitual tendencies, keeping our minds in secondary consciousness. I have understood that the path to taming distraction is found in stabilizing and strengthening the mind. If one can train the conceptual mind, one can attain wisdom. A good way to work with conception is to use the method of attaining calm by focusing, with the help of an object or without one. In both methods, being in the present moment is important, differentiated by the simple technique of acting as a vessel of transference in object meditation or acting as a witness in objectless meditation. This way, as seen in the illustration alongside, from the first act of placing the mind on the breath, continuing that placement, repeating that placement and staying close to the breath, we are able to transition past taming the mind and pacifying it (signified by the diminishing shade of the elephant, which represents our minds). After thoroughly pacifying the mind, we are able to be single-pointed. The distractions of the hare (lethargy) and monkey (agitation) disappear. It is said that when we attain perfect harmony of breath and being in the moment, our meditation is in a state of equanimity and from our hearts will flow a rainbow path. We will fly and hold the sword of perfect insight. I have particularly left the path till the ninth stage as undefined because I feel that there should be no absolute path to the pacification of the mind.

My favourite colour is blue and that is the colour my elephant ended up being!

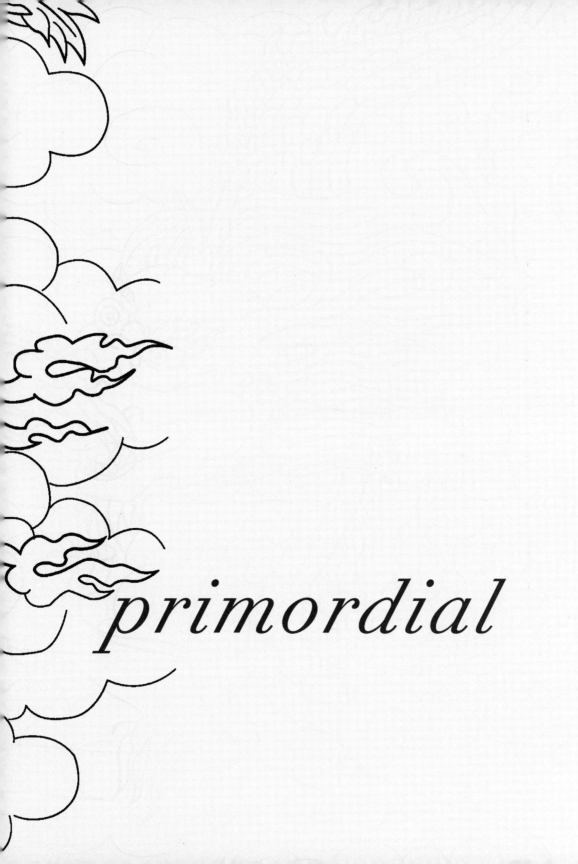

primordial

*D*ragons in Eastern cultures are different from what Western cultures consider them to be. The Dragon, in Buddhism, is a protector and one of the four supernatural animals of the four directions. Dragons are often used in Buddhist art and jewellery, finding cultural significance from their earliest reference in the Chinese Book of Changes (I Ching) where nine subspecies of dragons are listed. Dragons have many references worldwide, known commonly in the West as Draco, in Japan as Ryu-Jin and in Indian mythology as Vritra. My country, Bhutan, is known as Druk-Yul (land of the dragon), and we are called Drukpas. The dragon is also said to be the vehicle for Vairochana (The Primordial Buddha) himself. In this illustration, I have shown the dragon as being powerful and spread across the sky with the gentle flower of Vairochana, whom we are blessed to have among us in this lifetime in the reincarnated form of Vairochana Jigten Wangchuck Rinpoche.

atomic

peace

*T*he secret Tummo meditation practice is an advanced form of meditation that has been transmitted in the Vajrayana (Diamond Way) traditions of Tibetan Buddhism over the last millennium. Taken from the first of the six secret meditations of Naropa, Tummo has fascinated many of us. I do not wish to offer you a detailed description of my findings held sacred by followers, but I would like to share with you the ideal as I imagine it to be.

In this day and age, sentient beings all over the world are afflicted by the distractions of the last of the great yugas (ages). The age of kalyug or chaos as mentioned in the great Puranas is said to be the fourth and final era in the spiritual evolution cycle of humans. Societies are suffering great atrocities and injustices world over. The basis of the Tantric practice of Tummo, I imagine, is to seek epiphany through igniting the atomic energy that we are all said to have deep within us.

I have offered you a rock garden, the result of reaching your innermost energy, so that through any extreme conditions day and night, only peace will arise from you. This peace will be infectious and bring societies to understand true nature and co-existence.

lotus
born

uru Rinpoche (Padmasambhava) is said to have been miraculously born in the middle of a lake on a lotus flower, and he is widely venerated as the 'second Buddha' across the Himalayas. Padmasambhava is credited with introducing Buddhism to Bhutan and is the tutelary deity of this country. The famous Tiger's Nest monastery in Paro, Bhutan was built in the seventeenth century on the site around the cave, where Guru Rinpoche meditated for three years, three months, three weeks and three days when he visited Bhutan in the eighth century.

In 2005, I dreamt of many silhouetted and gigantic beings looking down from the cosmos. They were chanting 'Terton' (Treasure Revealer) repeatedly. So in the following years, I have rekindled my love for art and have since devoted most of my work to creating images of Guru Rinpoche in meditation using the *tsambhaka* flower.

the

great

fourth

*H*idden in the land of perfection, in the farthest reaches of the north-east of Bhutan is the Lion Fortress of Singye Dzong. Considered a most sacred place for pilgrimage, it is not a man-made monument like most Dzongs but a unique geological formation of mountains resembling a sleeping lion. In the nineteenth century, treasure revealer 'Terton' Zinon Namkha Dorji, discovered the 'Tse-Drup-Chimi-Sogthig' here, a holy scripture containing the way to prolong life.

The scripture is depicted alongside, as the jewels on the four elephants. This particular piece is dedicated to the long life of His Majesty The Fourth King of Bhutan, Jigme Singye Wangchuck.

peace

Garudas are common subjects of Buddhist and folk art throughout Asia. Statues of garudas often 'protect' temples and they were charged with protecting Mount Meru. The Buddha protected nagas from a garuda attack, earning both their followings. That is why I have depicted the garuda here holding a string of peaceful beads instead of a snake. Below the Garuda is the Kirtimukha, or 'glorious face'. The fierce monster face with huge fangs and a gaping mouth is quite common in the iconography of Indian and Southeast Asian temple architecture. The face is perhaps symbolic of our ego and pursuit of power and pleasure at the risk of destroying ourselves. From the mouth of this glorious face flow jewels to signify the fruit of longevity, which are gorged on by deer.

When I was a child I used to think
Of how the sun came to be.
The stars, I thought
Clustered for the day
To glow and never fall.
At night; sparkling spots of
A shattered soul.

musing

I chanced upon references to the Hindu creator, Brahma, and noticed many depictions of him as arising out of a lotus flower. The four Vedas are said to have come from the four heads of Brahma. This particular piece came together as a result of the prominence of both the garuda and Lord Brahma in Thailand and Indonesia. I was particularly charmed by the fact that this god never carries any weapons.

The environment is relative to energy,
consequent to action. It is reactive
to cause, catalytic to purpose and
metaphysically depreciative in the
abundance of care and carelessness.

love you back

*M*ount Meru is revisited with a hint of protection by its traditional guardian, the garuda, joined by the jewel holding limb of the dragon. The bows and arrows signify the clash of love and reciprocity in the cosmos. The illustration is supposed to give the colourist a sense of opposites culminating in the peace and beauty that the vase of flowers symbolizes in the foreground.

dharma queen

nspired by a famous twentieth-century Thangkha of the Gelugpa Assembly Tree, this version is my tribute to the compassion and benevolence of Her Majesty The Royal Grandmother of Bhutan. The sacred bell signifies a jewel-laden tree and the minister seated below offers Her Majesty the eight-faceted precious jewel. Buddhist stupas are designed in the likeness of the Buddha and thus the study illustrated in the background.

the triple
guard

The precursor to the raven crown of the Kings of Bhutan was the war-helmet crown of Jigme Namgyel, the Father of the First King of Bhutan. The raven is also an emanation of the guardian deity Mahakala, protector of the Dharma. Three lions are shown here, holding an offering of a flaming pearl.

On 5 February 2016, Prince Jigme Namgyel Wangchuck was born to His Majesty The King of Bhutan Jigme Khesar Namgyel Wangchuck and Her Majesty Jetsun Pema Wangchuck.

guru

A guru and his disciple were climbing a mountain when they came across an old woman struggling along the path. She asked the guru to help her. Ignoring the protests of his disciple, the guru insisted on carrying her on his back to her house. Hours later on their journey, the disciple finally approached his guru and voiced his displeasure at the old woman for making a senior monk carry her up the mountain.

The guru replied, 'I carried her till her house and put her down but you, my friend are still carrying her!'

This simple Zen story has a beautiful message about living and giving in the present moment.

I break from tradition here in this piece, by moving from the two-dimensional depictions of Buddhist iconography and art, to a subtle hint at three-dimensional harmony. Here, a dragon embraces the portal to Mount Meru.

Special Thanks

Special thanks to the knowledge and research
provided by the following:

David White (2011), Yoga in Practice

Alexander Studholme (2012), *The Origins of Om Manipadme Hum:
A Study of the Karandavyuha Sutra*, State University of New York Press

Access to Insight: a website dedicated to Theravada teachings

Ancient History Encyclopaedia

The Art of Living Foundation

Robert Beer's Encyclopaedia of Tibetan
Buddhist Symbols and Motifs